Contents

KU-224-744

Any words appearing in the text in bold, **like this**, are explained in the Glossary. You can also look out for them in the Word Bank at the bottom of each page.

Hiding in the shadows

Some criminals will do anything to get power or money. They might lie in wait to attack. Their **victim** might be someone who could make them feel powerful or make them rich. They will make careful plans before they **kidnap** or **assassinate** their victim.

History is full of kidnappers and assassins hiding in the shadows. They planned their attacks carefully. Some of them failed, but many did not. Some may still be out there.

Kidnappers wait in the shadows for their victims.

Word Bank   assassinate murder someone, such as a leader, by a secret attack

Kidnappers
AND Assassins

John Townsend

www.raintreepublishers.co.uk

Visit our website to find out more information about **Raintree** books.

To order:

 Phone 44 (0) 1865 888113

 Send a fax to 44 (0) 1865 314091

Visit the Raintree Bookshop at **www.raintreepublishers.co.uk** to browse our catalogue and order online.

First published in Great Britain by
Raintree, Halley Court, Jordan Hill, Oxford OX2 8EJ,
part of Harcourt Education.
Raintree is a registered trademark of Harcourt
Education Ltd.

Editorial: Melanie Copland and Sarah Chappelow
Design: Lucy Owen and Kamae Design
Picture Research: Hannah Taylor and Ginny Stroud-
Lewis
Production: Duncan Gilbert

Originated by RMW
Printed and bound in China
by South China Printing Company

10 digit ISBN 1 844 43811 2 (hardback)
13 digit ISBN 978 1 844 43811 2 (hardback)
11 10 09 08 07 06
10 9 8 7 6 5 4 3 2 1

10 digit ISBN 1 844 43817 1 (paperback)
13 digit ISBN 978 1 844 43817 4 (paperback)
12 11 10 09 08 07
10 9 8 7 6 5 4 3 2 1

British Library Cataloguing in Publication Data
Townsend, John
Kidnappers and Assassins. – (True Crime)
364.1'524
A full catalogue record for this book is available from
the British Library.

Acknowledgements
Alamy Images pp. title (Brand X Pictures), 8 (Jack
Sullivan); Associated Press pp. 30–31, 38–39; Corbis
pp. 36–37 (Bettmann), 20–21 (Bettmann), 20
(Bettmann), 22–23 (Bettmann), 22 (Bettmann), 23
(Joseph Sohm/ChromoSohm Inc.), 24 (Bettmann), 33
(Bettmann), 34 (Rick Friedman), 31 (Tim Graham);
Getty Images pp. 5 (Hulton Archive), 5 (Time Life
Pictures), 5 top (Hulton Archive), 7 (Hulton Archive),
10 (Hulton Archive), 11 top (Time Life Pictures), 11
bottom (Time Life Pictures), 12 (Hulton Archive), 13
(Hulton Archive), 12–13 (Hulton Archive), 14 (Hulton
Archive), 17 (Hulton Archive), 17 (Time Life Pictures),
18–19, 21 (Hulton Archive), 25 top (Time Life
Pictures), 25 bottom (Time Life Pictures), 26 (Hulton
Archive), 27 top (Hulton Archive), 27 bottom (Hulton
Archive), 30 (Hulton Archive), 32 (Hulton Archive),
32 (Hulton Archive), 34, 35 (Time Life Pictures), 38-39
(Stone), 41 (AFP), 42–43 (AFP); Harcourt Education
Ltd pp. 6 (Ginny Stroud-Lewis), 18 (Ginny Stroud-
Lewis), 44–45 (Ginny Stroud-Lewis); Mary Evans
Picture Library pp. 8–9, 15; NHPA p. 19 (Mark
Bowler); PA Photos p. 37; Rex Features pp. 16, 36, 38,
40; The Advertising Archive Ltd p. 28; The Art
Archive pp. 6–7 (Galleria d'Arte Moderna Rome/Dagli
Orti), 9; The Kobal Collection pp. 4–5 (London Films),
5 (Paramount), 14 (Warfield/United Artists), 41
(Dreamworks/Universal/Japp Buitendijk), 43
(Columbia); Topham Picturepoint p. 29.

Cover photograph of a gun sight reproduced with
permission of Corbis.

Every effort has been made to contact copyright
holders of any material reproduced in this book.
Any omissions will be rectified in subsequent
printings if notice is given to the publishers.

The paper used to print this book comes from
sustainable resources.

Surprise attack

People get kidnapped for all sorts of reasons. The kidnappers may want:

- money from the person's family
- a demand to be met, for example prisoners to be released
- to replace a child of their own that has died.

Like kidnapping, assassination starts with a surprise, secret attack. But kidnappers have something to gain from keeping their victims alive. This is not so with assassins. From the very start, they want their victims dead.

Once the assassin gets a victim in sight ... it can be deadly!

Find out later...

How did assassins start a war?

How did a kidnapper stun the United States?

How did a president survive an assassin?

kidnap carry off a person by force, or against his or her will
victim person who gets hurt or killed by crime

To change the world

Some people think the only way to make life better in their country is to get rid of the leader. A new leader might change things for the better. Many assassins in the past have tried to replace leaders in this way. Today most adults can vote to change their leaders. A vote in the **ballot** box is much better than a knife in the back! Italy is one country that had a few leaders who were **assassinated**.

Romans

2000 years ago, the Roman leaders and **emperors** had great power. No one would dare to argue with them. But some were prepared to kill them.

Can you believe it?

Being a Roman emperor was not always a good career. People with daggers and poisons were often waiting in the shadows. In just over 300 years, about 25 of Rome's emperors were assassinated. Sometimes the killer was someone who wanted to take over as emperor himself. It was a risky job!

Word Bank   ballot system of voting secretly
dictator person who rules on their own in a cruel way

Julius Caesar

In 44 BC the great Roman general Julius Caesar made himself Rome's leader. He expected to be treated like a king for the rest of his life. About 60 members of the **Senate** had other ideas. They plotted to get rid of him. The Roman Nicolaus of Damascus wrote this at the time:

> "All the men quickly raised their daggers and rushed at Caesar. Under the mass of wounds, he fell. Everyone wanted to have some part in the murder. There was not one of them who failed to strike his body as it lay there. Wounded thirty-five times, Caesar breathed his last breath and died."

Many people joined in on the assassination of Caesar.

The Second World War

Benito Mussolini (below) was a ruler with great power in Italy. In 1940, he declared war on the UK, France, the USSR, and the USA. But by 1945 many Italians had enough of this **dictator**. As he was trying to escape from Italy, he and some of his soldiers were shot. His body was hung up on a lamp post in Milan in front of the cheering crowds.

emperor ruler of an empire
Senate highest council of the ancient Roman Empire

The gunpowder plot

When England's Queen Elizabeth I died in 1603, English **Catholics** were pleased. They hoped the new King, James I, would be more **tolerant** of their religion. He was not! So, in 1605, a group of angry men decided to take action. They planned to blow up the king and his government. They hid 36 barrels of gunpowder in a cellar under the Houses of Parliament in London.

It was clear that innocent people would be killed in the attack. Some of the group had second thoughts. One of them warned his friend to stay away from Parliament on 5 November 1605. The king heard about the warning and took action.

If the plan had not failed, the gunpowder plot would have killed many people.

Word Bank

Catholics Christians of the Church led by the Pope
tolerant accepting the feelings and beliefs of others

Caught in the act

The king's soldiers quickly searched the buildings. They found one of the group – Guy Fawkes – hiding with the gunpowder in the cellar. He was taken away to be **tortured**. Soon the whole group was in prison. In a few months they were tried for **treason**. They were found guilty and put to death in early 1606. Within days, the failed assassins had been hanged in public as a warning to others. They were cut up and their insides were taken out. Their heads were stuck on poles and put on display.

Hung, drawn, and quartered

Guy Fawkes and his friends were punished for being **traitors**. It was a serious crime. Until 1870, traitors could get the same punishment as Guy Fawkes:

- dragged through streets to the place of **execution**
- hanged by the neck until almost dead
- cut open to have the insides taken out and burned (drawn)
- cut up into four parts (quartered).

This must have been a very painful way to die!

torture causing great pain to punish or to get information
treason harming your country or helping its enemies

Failed assassins

Through history there have been many assassination attempts. But quite a lot of them have failed. King Hussein of Jordan came to power because an assassin nearly killed him. In 1951, he was with his grandfather, who was the king. They were at a **mosque** when a gunman fired at the king. He was killed instantly. Fifteen-year-old Hussein was just steps away from him and one of the bullets hit him, too. Luckily the bullet hit a metal medal on his uniform, so he was not killed. Hussein took over as king when he was eighteen and ruled until his death in 1999.

King Hussein was very lucky to escape the assassin's bullet.

Word Bank   mosque Muslim place of worship

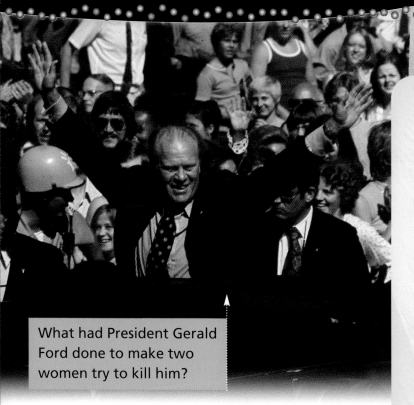

What had President Gerald Ford done to make two women try to kill him?

What a record!
The man to **survive** the most assassination attempts was the French president, Charles de Gaulle (below). In 22 years, there were 31 plots to kill him. None of them worked! In Paris, in 1962, gunmen wrecked his car with bullets. De Gaulle climbed out and said, "They really are bad shots."

Female assassins

Gerald Ford was president of the United States in the 1970s. In 1975, Lynette Fromme waited for him outside a California hotel. As he went to shake her hand, she pulled the trigger of her gun. It did not fire. Police grabbed her before she could pull the trigger again. Fromme was sentenced to life in prison.

Just over 2 weeks later, President Ford had another near miss. Sara Jane Moore pulled a gun from her handbag and fired from about 10 metres (33 feet) away. She missed! She, too, was sentenced to life in prison. President Ford was not hurt, just very lucky!

The start and end of wars

Some assassins hoped to stop a war, while others ended up starting one. Archduke Ferdinand was the son of the Emperor of Austria and Hungary. A gang of terrorists from Serbia attacked him in 1914. One shot at him from a window, but missed. Another threw a bomb, but only hit the car behind. A third, Gavrilo Princip, later ran right up to Ferdinand's car and shot him and his wife, who were both killed. Everyone was shocked by the assassination. In **revenge**, Austria attacked Serbia. This eventually led to the start of the First World War.

Archduke Ferdinand's assassination led to even worse things.

Lighting the fuse

Not many people know the name Gavrilo Princip. But his actions ended in the deaths of millions of people in the First World War. By **assassinating** Archduke Ferdinand, Princip caused Austria to attack Serbia. So the USSR attacked Austria. Then Germany, France, Italy, the UK, and the United States joined in.

Part of the Nazi headquarters was destroyed by the bomb.

Word Bank   Nazi Hitler's government in Germany from 1933 to 1945

The Second World War

On 20 July 1944, the **Nazi** leader Adolf Hitler had a meeting with his staff. Suddenly a briefcase exploded. The bomb killed four men and wrecked the whole room. But Hitler crawled out alive. The heavy oak table had shielded him from the blast.

The bomb had been planted by Claus von Stauffenberg, a German officer who no longer supported the Nazis. He wanted to bring the Second World War to an end. Unfortunately his plan failed. He and the other plotters were caught and he was shot dead later that day.

Assassin or hero?

Claus von Stauffenberg (below) became a hero of the Second World War. If he had managed to assassinate Hitler, the War would have ended sooner. Thousands of lives would have been saved. It was a risk that cost him his life.

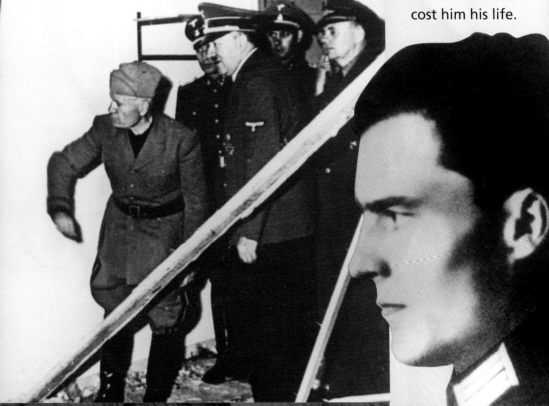

To change lives

Once upon a time...

Many old fairy stories scare children with tales of witches who steal children. They snatch them, carry them away and cook them! Another children's story, *Chitty Chitty Bang Bang*, has the dreaded Child Catcher (below) who creeps around looking for any child to throw into a cage!

Imagine you are asleep in your bed. Suddenly, a hand grabs your face. You are pulled from your bed and dragged away into the night. You may never see your home again. Scenes like this were common in Roman times. There was a demand for slaves. Anyone could be taken away and sold.

Later, pirate gangs would **kidnap** people from ships or from seaside towns in Europe and sell them as slaves across the world. They could strike at any time and snatch you from your bed…

Slavery was once very common.

Word Bank   illegal against the law
impostor person who pretends to be someone else

Press gangs

Kidnapping was once **legal**! How did the British Navy get men to sail all its ships? They sent **press gangs** to kidnap any men they could find. Press gangs would take almost anyone. The 1700s were dangerous times.

Last week a man going over Black-Heath met four men who press-ganged him. He begged them to let him go as his family would starve without him. They agreed to let him go if he gave them money. But soon another gang grabbed him. He begged them and told them what had just happened. They went to find the first gang, which had been **impostors.** They caught them and press-ganged the lot!

Slavery

A slave is a person who is taken and "owned" by someone else. Kidnapping people to sell as slaves was once very common around the world. Slavery was banned in many countries in the 1800s. The UK stopped slave trading in 1833. Slaves were set free in the United States in 1865. Slavery is **illegal** in all countries today.

Press gangs were a common sight in the 1700s.

legal allowed by law
press gang navy gang that took men away to become sailors

The police used this information to search for Patty Hearst.

Patricia Campbell Hearst
FBI No. 325,805 L10
Date photograph taken unknown
Alias: Tania
Age: 20, born February 20, 1954, San Francisco, California
Height: 5'3"
Eyes: Brown
Weight: 110 pounds
Complexion: Fair
Build: Small
Race: White
Hair: Light brown
Nationality: American
Scars and Marks: Mole on lower right corner of mouth, scar near right ankle
Remarks: Hair naturally light brown, straight and worn about three inches below shoulders in length, however, may wear wigs, including Afro style, dark brown of medium length; was last seen wearing black sweater, plaid slacks, brown hiking boots and carrying a knife in her belt

CAUTION

THE ABOVE INDIVIDUALS ARE SELF-PROCLAIMED MEMBERS OF THE SYMBIONESE LIBERATION ARMY AND REPORTEDLY HAVE BEEN IN POSSESSION OF NUMEROUS FIREARMS INCLUDING AUTOMATIC WEAPONS. WILLIAM HARRIS AND PATRICIA HEARST AL-LEGEDLY HAVE RECENTLY USED GUNS TO AVOID ARREST. ALL THREE SHOULD BE CONSIDERED ARMED AND VERY DANGEROUS.

Federal warrants were issued on May 20, 1974, at Los Angeles, California, charging the Harris' and Hearst with violation of the National Firearms Act. Hearst was also charged in a Federal complaint on April 15, 1974, at San Francisco, California, as a material witness to a bank robbery which occurred April 15, 1974.

IF YOU HAVE ANY INFORMATION CONCERNING THESE PERSONS, PLEASE NOTIFY ME OR CONTACT YOUR LOCAL FBI OFFICE. TELEPHONE NUMBERS AND ADDRESSES OF ALL FBI OFFICES LISTED ON BACK.

CmKelley

The SLA

The SLA was a small group of young people who hated the rich. They wanted to change the way the world thought about money. That was why they kidnapped Patty Hearst in 1974. Her family was a **symbol** of the wealthy United States.

Kidnapped and brainwashed

Some kidnaps are very unusual and have strange endings. In 1974, Patty Hearst was 19 years old. Her grandfather was a rich and famous **publisher**. Patty was **kidnapped** at gunpoint when three people burst into her home in Berkeley, USA. The story was headline news around the world. A criminal group called SLA (Symbionese Liberation Army) sent a demand to Patty's father. If he wanted to see her again, he had to pay millions of dollars for food to be given to the poor. He did all he was asked and waited for Patty's safe return. There was no more news. Patty's family feared the worst.

Word Bank   brainwash encouraging someone to change their ideas, sometimes by force

A sudden change

Two months later, an amazing story hit the news. There had been a bank robbery in San Francisco. The bank's camera showed one of the robbers clearly. It was Patty Hearst. Her family had already received tapes from the SLA. In these Patty spoke to them about how she had changed. She now hated her parents and their money. She had joined the SLA's fight to make a better world. They robbed to feed the poor.

A month later, the police found the SLA's hideout and burned it down. Patty was arrested in 1975. She was sent to prison for 7 years for armed robbery.

Patty's defence

Patty claimed she had been forced to join the SLA. They had **brainwashed** her. She said:
- she was made to feel that no one was going to rescue her
- she was told she might die
- she was told lies about her family and country
- she was forced to record tapes blaming her family.

Patty was just 19 years old when she was kidnapped.

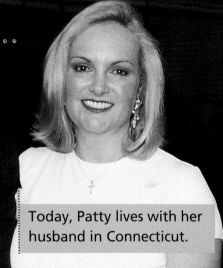

Today, Patty lives with her husband in Connecticut.

symbol something or someone that stands for something else

Animal napping

Stealing people's animals to eat or sell is a very old crime. **Kidnapping** an animal to hold it for **ransom** is very unusual, though. This happened to Shergar, a famous prize-winning racehorse in Ireland. Horse thieves "kidnapped" Shergar in 1983.

Pets for bills!

If you do not pay your bills in eastern Russia, your pet could be kidnapped. "We will take away your dog till you pay up," a gas company said to customers. Russian police say it is not **illegal** to **seize** property such as pets if people owe money. The kidnapped pets are sold if their owners still do not pay.

POLICE HUNT SHERGAR'S KIDNAPPERS

(8 February 1983)

A hunt for the UK Derby winner Shergar has begun in Ireland. The prize horse was kidnapped from stables in County Kildare. At least six kidnappers told the head **groom** they would phone a ransom demand. The horse is said to be worth £10 million.

Word Bank   **groom** person who looks after a horses

Horse mystery

Masked gunmen took Shergar from his stable at night. They later demanded £2 million to return the horse. The problem was that many people owned Shergar. It took them all a long time to agree what to do. While they were trying to get the ransom money together, suddenly everything went quiet. Nothing was ever heard from the horse thieves again.

To this day, no one is really sure what became of Shergar. Perhaps he was killed or perhaps he lived the rest of his days in a field somewhere. Who knows?

We will probably never know what really happened to Shergar.

Kidnappers in the wild

An orang-utan is a type of ape. Some female orang-utans have been seen stealing baby orang-utans from their mothers. Sometimes they bring them up themselves; sometimes they give them back after a little while. Some types of adult ape have been known to kidnap and kill the babies of other apes.

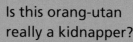

Is this orang-utan really a kidnapper?

---

ransom payment for the release of someone who is kidnapped
seize find and take

The cost of leadership

The problem with being a president is that everyone knows who you are and where you go. This can include dangerous and violent people. Such people have set out to kill US presidents through history.

President Lincoln

Abraham Lincoln was the sixteenth US president. In 1865, he and his wife went to watch a play in Washington, D.C. John Wilkes Booth, an actor who once performed at the theatre, crept up behind the president. He pulled out a pistol, shot Lincoln in the head, and killed him. Booth then leapt on to the stage and fled into the night. Soldiers later found him and shot him dead.

President Abraham Lincoln.

Angry assassin

The American **Civil War** in the 1860s was a tough time for President Abraham Lincoln. John Wilkes Booth was angry at the result of the war and blamed the president. That was why he set out to get his **revenge** at a theatre one night. It was a night that went down in US history.

John Wilkes Booth was Lincoln's assassin.

Word Bank   civil war war fought between people living in the same country

President Garfield

James Garfield was the twentieth US president and the second to be **assassinated**. He died only a few months after becoming president.

Charles Guiteau was a lawyer. He gave speeches in support of the president and wanted an important job at the White House as a reward. His request was turned down. Guiteau was so angry he decided to shoot the president. On 2 July 1881 he fired a gun at the president. The bullet lodged in James Garfield's back and doctors could not remove it. He died a few weeks later. Guiteau was found guilty of murder and hanged in 1882.

President McKinley

The third US president to be assassinated was William McKinley in 1901. Leon Czolgosz shot him twice. The assassin was found guilty and sent to the electric chair. His last words were "I killed the president because he was the enemy of the good working people. I am not sorry for my crime."

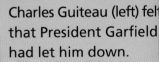
Charles Guiteau (left) felt that President Garfield had let him down.

Kennedy

John F. Kennedy was the 35th president of the United States. He was a popular president. His assassination in November 1963 stunned the world. He was shot in Dallas, Texas, in front of crowds as he rode in the back of a convertible limo. As he fell forward with a severe head wound, the limo sped off to Parkland Hospital. John Kennedy was declared dead and the news swept across the United States and the world. People wept in the streets and a shocked world asked "why?" To this day, there are many ideas about what happened in Dallas that day.

About John F. Kennedy...

Term of office:
20 January 1961 to 22 November 1963
Took over from:
President Dwight D. Eisenhower
Replaced by:
Lyndon Johnson
Date of birth:
29 May 1917
Place of birth:
Brookline, Massachusetts
Date of death:
22 November 1963
Place of death:
Dallas, Texas
Wife: Jacqueline Lee Bouvier
Political party:
Democrat

President Kennedy was shot just after this picture was taken.

Mystery assassin

Lee Harvey Oswald was 24 years old. The police said he shot Kennedy with a rifle from a window on the sixth floor of a warehouse where he worked. He then ran off and shot dead a policeman. He was arrested later at a nearby theatre. He swore he was innocent.

Was Oswald really the killer? People still wonder. Was he a secret agent? He could never tell his story as he, too, was shot dead, during a prison transfer. Jack Ruby said he shot him for **revenge**. Some people say it was to stop Oswald telling who had ordered him to shoot the president. Ruby went to prison where he died a few years later.

Strange but true

- Both President Lincoln and President Kennedy were assassinated on a Friday.
- After their deaths, men called Johnson replaced both of them as president.
- Lincoln's killer shot him in a theatre and ran to a warehouse. Kennedy's killer shot him from a warehouse and ran to a theatre.

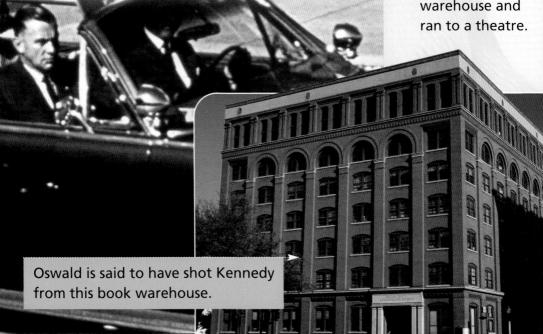

Oswald is said to have shot Kennedy from this book warehouse.

The assassin's gun

In the 1960s, there were many problems in the United States. The **Civil Rights Movement** was fighting for African Americans to be treated fairly. One of its leaders was Martin Luther King. He gave powerful speeches to encourage African Americans in their struggle. He was against violence and led peaceful protests. Some white people hated what he was doing. One of them was James Earl Ray. He **confessed** to shooting Martin Luther King dead in 1968. He was sent to prison, where he died in 1998.

Always remembered

Many people think that Martin Luther King (below) was one of the greatest leaders and heroes in the United States's history. Martin Luther King Day is now celebrated on the third Monday in January each year in the United States.

Martin Luther King tried to get equal rights for black people.

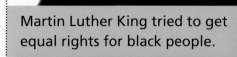

Word Bank   Civil Rights Movement organized group taking
action for equal rights for people of all races

Another Kennedy

President John F. Kennedy had a younger brother called Robert. He, too, was hoping to become president of the United States in 1968. He had just won the first stage in the race to become president. As he and his team were celebrating, one of the men at the party – Sirhan Sirhan – shot him. Sirhan was pulled to the ground by the crowd. At first he confessed to the shooting, but later he **denied** it. Robert Kennedy died the next day. Sirhan was found guilty of murder and was sent to prison for life.

Malcolm X was a famous speaker for African American rights.

Robert Kennedy's shooting turned his party into chaos.

Malcolm X

Malcolm X made many speeches on behalf of African Americans in the USA. He broke away from a black rights organization to lead his own group. This upset some people who felt he had **betrayed** them. In New York in 1965, three gunmen killed Malcolm. They shot him 15 times. His assassins were **convicted** of murder.

betray to act against your friends or country
confess admit to doing something wrong

20th-century kidnaps

Many kidnappers have been at work in the last 100 years for all kinds of reasons. Some of the reasons are still a mystery.

Star of the 1920s

Charles Lindbergh (below) was a hero. In 1927, he was the first man to fly a plane alone across the Atlantic. The United States loved him and called him Lucky Lindy. When he married his millionaire wife, the papers were full of his story. Tragedy struck when their son was kidnapped.

The missing baby

In the United States in the 1930s, a big story hit the news. It sent a shock wave across the world. A terrible crime hit the famous Lindbergh family. On the night of 1 March 1932, their baby boy Chas went missing. Police found a ladder against his window. A kidnapper had crept into the room where the baby slept. A **ransom** note told his parents to pay US$50,000 for his safe return.

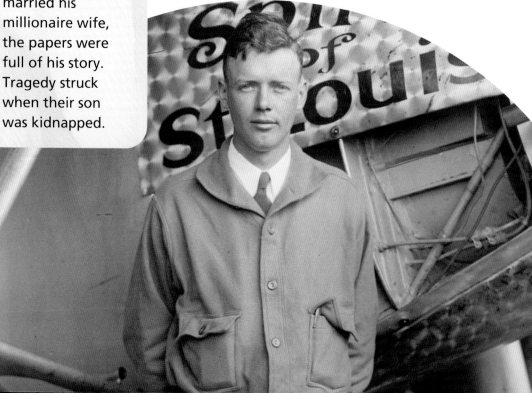

Nobody really knows what happened to Chas Lindbergh

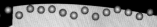

Remaining mystery

The police were never really sure about the body they found in the woods. This was before **DNA testing** was even thought of. In fact, the body was thought to be bigger than little Chas Lindbergh. Many people think the real baby grew up and is alive today. Some people claim to be him!

Kidnapper or victim?

Everyone searched for the missing baby. Charles Lindbergh paid the US$50,000 ransom, but nothing happened. Two months later, police found a dead baby in nearby woods. Bruno Hauptmann was arrested and found guilty of kidnapping and murdering Chas. Hauptmann was put to death.

Some questions remain about the case. Many people think Hauptmann was not guilty at all. They think there was more to this crime. Some even think the kidnap story was made up to hide a killer in the family. The case of the missing baby will remain one of the great crime stories of last century.

Was Bruno Hauptmann innocent?

DNA testing scientific way of proving whether two people are related to each other

All for money

Some children have been **kidnapped** because their parents are very rich. Their kidnappers may be cruel. Other kidnappers have looked after their **victims** very well.

In 1960, the owner of the French car company Peugeot was Raymond Peugeot. This millionaire had a 4-year-old son, Eric. One morning Eric disappeared. His kidnappers told Raymond to pay a **ransom** of £18,000. If not, he would never see his son again. He paid up and Eric was returned safe and well. His two kidnappers were found and arrested in 1962. They were both sentenced to 20 years in prison.

The wealth earned from Peugeot cars made Raymond's family a target for kidnappers.

Graeme Thorne

It was also 1960 when a more tragic kidnapping took place. It was the first of its kind in Australia. Bazil and Freda Thorne won £100,000 in the Sydney lottery. That was a lot in 1960. Their story was in all the papers. Soon afterwards, their 8-year-old son Graeme vanished on his way to school. A man phoned his parents and asked for a ransom of £25,000. The Thornes paid up, but then heard no more.

A month or so later, Graeme's body was found tied up in a rug. Stephen Bradley, one of the men that the police questioned, left the country in a hurry. They went after him and charged him with Graeme's murder. With the help of **forensic** evidence he was found guilty and sent to prison.

Proof

Forensic evidence linked Stephen Bradley to Graeme Thorne's body. **Fibres** from the rug around Graeme's body were found in Bradley's car. The reason Bradley killed him was never discovered.

The kidnapping of Graeme Thorne ended in tragedy

Ransom demands

John Paul Getty III was in his teens in 1973 when he was **kidnapped** in Rome, Italy. His grandfather was a famous oil billionaire, but refused to pay the kidnapper's demand of US$17 million. Then, an envelope arrived. Inside was a lock of hair ... and an ear. A note said:

> This is John Paul's ear. If we don't get money in 10 days, the other ear will arrive. He will arrive bit by bit.

John Paul was set free after his grandfather paid a large sum of money. He needed treatment for his missing ear. His kidnappers were thought to be in the Italian **mafia**, but were never found.

Scarred for life

Despite being born into one of the richest families in the world, John Paul Getty III (below) did not have an easy time. Kidnappers cut off his ear and kept him locked up for weeks. He never really recovered from his **ordeal**. He turned to drugs, which wrecked his health. He had a **stroke**, became disabled, and almost blind.

Word Bank mafia large organized group of criminals
ordeal terrible experience

The Chowchilla kidnap

In the United States in 1976, a bus full of 5- to 14-year-olds disappeared. They were returning to Chowchilla, California, after a swimming trip and were travelling on a country road in Madera County. The empty bus was found in a ditch. The driver, along with nineteen girls and seven boys, had been locked in a truck buried in a quarry. After 16 hours underground, the **victims** managed to dig their way out and all escaped.

The son of the quarry owner was missing with two of his friends. He had left behind a **ransom** note demanding US$5 million. Police hunted the men and arrested them. All three were found guilty and sent to prison for life.

Amazingly, 27 people escaped from this buried truck.

Kidnap attempt on Princess Anne (1974)

As a car near Buckingham Palace blocked Princess Anne's Rolls Royce, six shots were fired. A man tried to get into her car, but Princess Anne's detective wounded him. The Princess was shocked, but not hurt. Ian Ball, 26, had sent a letter to the Queen demanding £3 million for Anne's release. His plan failed and he was sentenced to life in prison.

stroke sudden illness caused when blood cannot reach the brain

Many kidnappings and **assassinations** were in the news in the 1980s. Some of the **victims** were children. Others were famous adults.

New York – 1980

John Lennon became famous as a singer and songwriter with The Beatles in the 1960s. With Paul McCartney, he wrote some of the best-known songs of the 1960s. When The Beatles split up, he moved to live in New York.

One night in 1980, an **obsessive** fan waited for him outside his home in the Dakota Building. John Lennon was shot and killed.

The world was shocked by Lennon's sudden death.

No reason

John Lennon was 40 when Mark Chapman shot and killed him. Although he was a fan and had just spoken to John, Chapman had a mental illness and was not thinking normally. He could not say why he killed his hero.

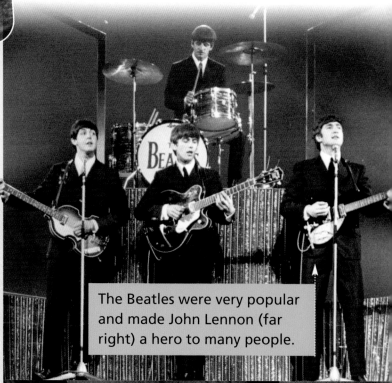

The Beatles were very popular and made John Lennon (far right) a hero to many people.

Word Bank   obsessive always thinking or worrying about something

The assassin

This is the statement of Mark David Chapman to police at 1 a.m. on 9 December 1980, 3 hours after he had murdered John Lennon:

"I went to the building. It's called the Dakota. I stayed there until John Lennon came out and I asked him to sign my album. I waited until he came back again in a car. John looked at me. I took the gun from my coat pocket and fired at him. I can't believe I could do that. I didn't want to run away. I don't know what happened to the gun. Then the police came and told me to put my hands on the wall and cuffed me."

Life sentence

In 2000, after serving 20 years in prison for murder, Mark Chapman was considered for **parole**. He was turned down.

"It's a horrible thing to realize what you've done"

(Mark Chapman, 2000)

His parole was turned down again in 2002 and 2004.

Mark Chapman during his court case.

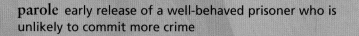

parole early release of a well-behaved prisoner who is unlikely to commit more crime

There was panic when President Reagan was shot.

Horror film

From 1981 to 1989 Ronald Reagan (below) was president of the United States. Years before, he had acted in films. But he was in a very different kind of film that was watched in horror across the world. He was shot in front of a crowd. He later joked to his wife, "Honey, I forgot to duck!"

Narrow escapes – 1981

Two very famous men were almost **assassinated** in 1981. One was president of the United States and the other was the **Pope**.

Ronald Reagan had been president of the United States for only a few months when he gave a speech at a Washington hotel. As he left, 25-year-old John Hinckley shot him. Four men were wounded, including the president. He had a bad chest wound that almost killed him. Hinckley was caught on the spot. Doctors said that he was **insane**, and sent him to a high-security mental hospital. Ronald Reagan recovered and was president for another 8 years. He died in his nineties in 2004.

Word Bank   insane having terrible mental problems
intestines part of the body that helps to digest food

Pope John Paul II

John Paul II became Pope in 1978. He went on to be the third longest-serving Pope. This nearly did not happen. As he entered St Peter's Square in Rome, Italy, on 13 May 1981, there were sudden gunshots from the crowd. John Paul II was shot. He was rushed to hospital. He needed emergency surgery to remove part of his **intestines**. His hand was also hurt. Fortunately, he made a full recovery and even visited his attacker in prison 2 years later. From then on, the Pope always travelled in a car with bulletproof glass.

Behind bars

The man who tried to assassinate John Paul II was a member of a Turkish terrorist group. His name was Agca and he hated the Roman Catholic religion. He was sent to prison for life in Italy, but was released in 2000. He returned to Turkey where he killed a man and was soon back behind bars.

This special Popemobile has bulletproof glass.

pope head of the Roman Catholic Church

John Walsh tries to help catch criminals.

Boys taken

Six-year-old Adam Walsh lived with his parents in Florida, USA. One day in 1981 he and his mother were out shopping. She let him play a video game while she paid for her shopping. When she got back, Adam was not where she had left him. After a **frantic** search, the police were called. They could not find Adam either. Posters and television programmes asked for help, but no one knew where he was. Two weeks later, Adam's head was found in a canal 190 kilometres (120 miles) away from where he was **kidnapped**. His body was never found. The story shocked the whole country.

America's Most Wanted

The kidnapper of Adam Walsh has never been found. John Walsh, Adam's father, spoke a lot about the crime on television. He became a well-known television presenter on crime matters. His television show *America's Most Wanted* has helped to catch many criminals across the United States.

Adam Walsh's parents asked for help to find his killer.

Word Bank   frantic wild and hurried, in a panic

Ben Needham

Ben was born in 1989. His kidnappers struck nearly 2 years later. He had gone with his grandparents to stay on the Greek Island of Kos. They last saw him playing in the garden.
One minute he was there, the next he had gone. They searched all around, but there was no sign of Ben. The police could not find him anywhere. They had no clues about who had taken him away. Ben would be a teenager now. Every year people say they see him or know where he is. So far, he has not been found.

Have you seen Ben?

Ben Needham's parents hope that someone will find him somewhere one day. But they cannot be sure what he looks like now. Police artists have used pictures of Ben from when he was a baby to show what he may have looked like at 14 years of age (below).

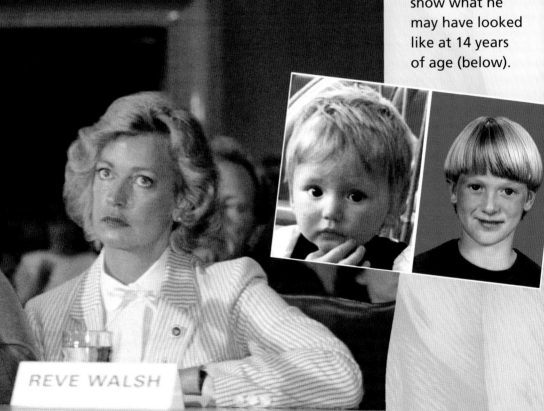

REVE WALSH

Kidnappers named

In 2001, 49-year-old Brian Mitchell (below) did some work on a house in Salt Lake City, USA. It was where Elizabeth Smart lived. The following year Elizabeth disappeared. It seems that Mitchell took her to become his second wife. According to the television show *America's Most Wanted*, his first wife – Wanda Barzee – helped with the **kidnap**.

Kidnappers and assassins are still out there. They have been at work over the last few years planning some terrible crimes.

A shocking news story in 2002 told of a 14-year-old girl who was snatched from her own home in Salt Lake City, Utah, USA. A man broke in and took Elizabeth Smart from the bedroom she shared with her younger sister. Many people helped the police to search streets and countryside, but there was no sign of her anywhere. The news story gripped the nation. Many people feared Elizabeth would never be found alive.

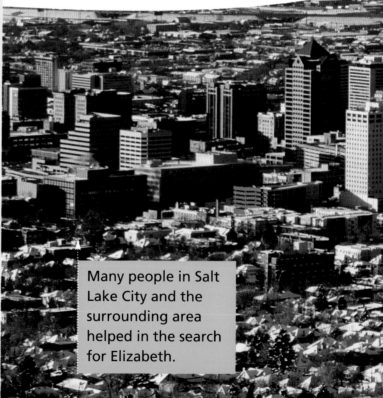

Many people in Salt Lake City and the surrounding area helped in the search for Elizabeth.

Word Bank   accused blamed for doing wrong

Good news

Nine months later the police got a call. They rushed to the scene and found Elizabeth safe and well. It was in March 2003 that someone saw three strange people in a street in Sandy, Utah. This was just 24 kilometres (15 miles) from Elizabeth Smart's home. One of the people was wearing a dark wig. It was Elizabeth! A **drifter** man and woman had been holding her against her will. They were quickly arrested and Elizabeth was back with her family at last.

Salt Lake City, 2004

A judge says the woman **accused** of Elizabeth Smart's kidnapping is still not well enough to stand trial. Wanda Barzee has been sent back to a state hospital for another year of mental treatment.

drifter someone with no real home or fixed address

Plot to kidnap Victoria Beckham

A gang planned to kidnap the family of the football star David Beckham in 2002. His wife, Victoria Beckham, and their son were to be held for a £5 million ransom. Five men were charged with planning the kidnap. In court, the case was dropped after the judge said a key **witness** was not to be trusted.

The cost of fame

In the last few years, many famous people have had to hire 24-hour security guards. The cost of their fame is that they are at constant risk. Gangs could **kidnap** them and demand high **ransoms** to set them free. Some **insurance** companies now include kidnap and ransom – known as K&R – in their services. This business is worth millions of pounds each year.

A number of famous people have also had death threats. So life as a star these days is not always that safe.

The Beckhams' fame and wealth make them a target for greedy kidnappers.

Word Bank

ceremony special event
FBI United States's Federal Bureau of Investigation

Russell Crowe

In 2001, the **FBI** heard there was a plot to kidnap the film star Russell Crowe. It was feared the 36-year-old actor would be snatched from a film award **ceremony**. Security guards surrounded Crowe. FBI agents were also keeping a close eye on him. In the end, nothing happened.

In fact, Russell Crowe had even played the part of a kidnap expert in a film called *Proof of Life*. Real life became scarier than the film. A friend of Russell Crowe said, "We're all aware of the kidnap plot and the FBI has been guiding us. Russell has now taken many security **precautions**."

Tennis star at risk (2004)

Russian teenager Maria Sharapova may be a kidnap target. Maria won the women's Wimbledon title in 2004 and has lived in the United States since she was eight. Many of her family are in Russia, where sports players have been kidnapped before. A friend said, "Her new fame means she must take care. Leading sports people are now targets for **ruthless** gangs."

Russell Crowe was nearly the **victim** of a real-life kidnap.

insurance promise to pay money to someone if their property is damaged, or if they are harmed

Troubled times

How do you make world leaders do what you want? Some people think violence is the only way. They **assassinate** or **kidnap** to get what they want. Kidnapping someone can be seen as a way to make leaders listen and act. In recent times, there have been a number of **political** kidnaps.

After the United States and UK entered Iraq in 2003, some Iraqis were angry at being ruled by foreign soldiers. The only way they felt they could be heard was to kidnap and assassinate people. They sent a strong message: "Do what we say … or else!"

Armed pirates attack two tugboats and kidnap crew (Oct. 2004)

With guns blazing, pirates have robbed boats in the Malacca Strait, Singapore. The pirates, thought to be Indonesians, robbed the crew of valuables and maps. They took away the captain and engineer but left the rest of the sailors unharmed. As yet, there is no news of their prisoners.

Even though the war in Iraq is over, it can still be a dangerous place.

Word Bank   abduction snatch a person away by force, like kidnapping
distress great worry and mental suffering

Iraq

Hundreds of foreign workers were kidnapped in Iraq after the war. Many were killed. Some kidnappers wanted the United States and UK to leave Iraq. Some wanted Iraqi prisoners to be set free. Others just wanted money. The British man Ken Bigley was held hostage in October 2004 and made to appear on television. The world waited for news of him. Sadly, the kidnappers killed Ken Bigley after he tried to escape.

Kidnappers and assassins will always try to get what they want. Their actions cause great **distress** for many. It will take even more effort to make sure their crimes fail in the future.

Do you believe in aliens?

Are you safe?

Thousands of people say they have been kidnapped ... by aliens! Some people say that alien **abductions** are on the rise. Scientists have studied people who say they have been kidnapped by aliens. They tend to suffer from bad sleep patterns, and often believe in a **fantasy** world.

fantasy not real, made up
political beliefs about power and how to run countries

Find out more

44

Kidnaps and weddings

The tradition of a bride asking her closest friends to be bridesmaids dates back to ancient times. Maids would dress like the bride to confuse evil spirits who might try to **kidnap** her.

If you want to find out more about the criminal underworld, why not have a look at these books:

Behind the Scenes: Solving a Crime,
    Peter Mellet (Heinemann Library, 1999)
Forensic Files: Investigating Murders,
    Paul Dowswell (Heinemann Library, 2004)
Forensic Files: Investigating Thefts and Heists,
    Alex Woolf (Heinemann Library, 2004)
Just the Facts: Cyber Crime,
    Neil McIntosh (Heinemann Library, 2002)

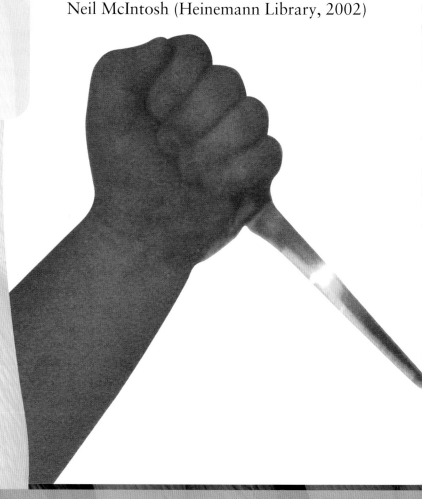

Did you know?

- The term "kid nabbing" began in England. **Abduction** of children to harm them, or for **ransom**, only became known in the United States from the 1880s. During the 1920s, a series of kidnappings became big news stories and scared parents across the United States.

- An English king, King Edmund 'Ironside', met a nasty end. He was killed while sitting on a wooden toilet. An assassin was hiding in the pit below. He twice thrust his sword up the king's rear end. He met his end in every way!

- The only British Prime Minister to be **assassinated** was Spencer Perceval. Henry Bellingham shot him dead in the House of Commons and was hanged for the crime in 1812.

Kidnap facts

In 2001, the FBI handled 93 cases of children being **kidnapped** by strangers:

- in over 85 per cent of the cases, the **victim** was kept within 80 kilometres (50 miles) of where he or she was kidnapped
- the kidnapped children were returned safely in just over half of the cases.

Glossary

abduction snatch a person away by force, like kidnapping

accused blamed for doing wrong

assassinate murder someone, such as a leader, by a secret attack

ballot system of voting secretly

betray to act against your friends or country

brainwash encouraging someone to change their ideas, sometimes by force

Catholics Christians of the Church led by the Pope

ceremony special event

Civil Rights Movement organized group taking action for equal rights for people of all races

civil war war fought between people living in the same country

confess admit to doing something wrong

convicted found guilty in a court of law

denied not admitting to doing wrong

dictator person who rules on their own, often in a cruel way

distress great worry and mental suffering

DNA testing scientific way of proving whether two people are related to each other

drifter someone with no real home or fixed address

emperor ruler of an empire

execution put to death

fantasy not real, made up

FBI United States's Federal Bureau of Investigation

fibres tiny threads

forensic scientific investigation to help solve crimes

frantic wild and hurried, in a panic

groom person who looks after a horses

illegal against the law

impostor person who pretends to be someone else

insane having terrible mental problems

insurance promise to pay money to someone if their property is damaged, or if they are harmed

intestines part of the body that helps to digest food

kidnap carry off a person by force, or against his or her will

legal allowed by law

mafia large organized group of criminals

mosque Muslim place of worship

Nazi Hitler's government in Germany from 1933 to 1945

obsessive always thinking or worrying about something

ordeal terrible experience

parole early release of a well-behaved prisoner who is unlikely to commit more crime

political beliefs about power and how to run countries

pope head of the Roman Catholic Church

precaution care taken before an event to stop harm

press gang navy gang that took men away to become sailors

publisher person who runs a company that makes books

ransom payment for the release of someone who is kidnapped

revenge get even with someone

ruthless cruel

seize find and take

Senate highest council of the ancient Roman Empire

stroke sudden illness caused when blood cannot reach the brain

survive continue to live

symbol something or someone that stands for something else

tolerant accepting the different feelings and beliefs of others

torture causing great pain to punish or to get information

traitor someone who betrays another person's trust – or their own country

treason crime of harming your country or of helping its enemies

victim person who gets hurt or killed by crime

witness someone who is there when something happens

Index